The Art and Practice of Transformational Leadership

Leading with Purpose and Presence

DR. SACKEENA GORDON-JONES

Editor: Rachel Wynne

ISBN: 1519778139
ISBN-13:978-1519778130

DEDICATION

This book is dedicated to my mother,
Jeanne Gordon,
Who had a choice, and decided that she would give life.

Also, to my Husband, Tony, my beloved;
And my daughters, Brittny and Monique,
Whose continued support and love replenish my soul.

CONTENTS

ACKNOWLEDGMENTS

Over the years, I have learned about leadership from being in the trenches and from paying attention to the amazing leaders of my lifetime. A dear friend, Joe Mangum, once said: You can be taught in two ways: "seeing what's right" and "seeing what's wrong"; I have had the opportunity to gain from both types of learning experiences.

I am thankful for the mentors in my life, who have provided me support by witnessing me and sharing feedback, insight and wisdom. Myles Monroe helped me understand the power of potential and purpose. Ed Page, your counsel and support let me know that my playing small wouldn't serve my organization or me.

Special thanks to father, GC, and my siblings: Hugh, Yvette, La-Tanya and Venice, for your continuous encouragement and support; which has fueled me to finish line. Also to my colleagues in the 'Write Rite' group, and especially to Ray Wynne, for her time and effort in editing the work.

ACKNOWLEDGMENTS

"Transformational Leaders serve two crucial purposes: To awaken our consciousness, and inspire us to action"

-Sackeena Gordon-Jones

WHY IS TRANSFORMATIONAL LEADERSHIP SO IMPORTANT?

Transformational Leadership is essential, to impel us toward consciousness. It awakens us to what could be: in us, through us and around us. It calls us toward better; spiritually and personally first, then socially and organizationally. Transformational Leadership is defined as a style of leadership where the leader is charged with identifying the needed change, creating a vision to guide the change by inspiring, and executing the change in tandem with committed members of the group. I believe the essence of this is: seeing what needs to be, becoming the example of it, and in so doing, breathing life into the vision. This inspires other to join in and own the vision, so that moving towards it, literally transforms the followers and the community through a ripple effect.

Transformational Leadership yields change with a purpose. A change that is ennobling. No change occurs without there being awareness of a desired state or situation that is better than the current state or situation. This awareness must be coupled with a sense that the promise of the desired state is more compelling than the comfort or pain of the current state. We refer to this sense as a "Burning Platform". The phrase comes from a story of a man at sea. A man is out on the North Atlantic Ocean on an oil platform. One night an explosion wakes him. He sees a growing fire on the platform. Striving to escape the impending flames, he is able to find his way through the chaos to the edge of the platform. As the fire heartlessly approaches him he must decide to take radical action and risk his life or choose to do nothing, which could lead to a horrible death. His option for a better state is to jump more than 100 feet from the fire-ridden platform into the freezing North Atlantic waters. If the dangerous jump does not kill him, he could die from exposure within minutes if not rescued. He made the decision; he jumped! Fortunately, the man did survive the jump from the platform and he was rescued by a boat crew. The story emphasizes that we are driven to take radical action to change our state, when it is more painful to remain in our current state. We sense we're on a 'burning platform'. Thus, change becomes more compelling. A Transformational Leader helps awaken our consciousness to our state, and the potential of our fate, if we resist a meaningful change. Without this awakening to a current and or possible state, we may miss our possibilities and abort our potential. What is clear and eminent is that the status quo is not an option. Some have said, that if I just stay the course, stand without moving forward, then I am no worse off. However, the truth is that if we stand where we are, while others are moving forward, we are really falling behind or regressing. Take for example, the businessperson who resists getting a smart phone. At first, people are patient with him/her. However, if the business person does not change and get connected with a smart phone, it will not take long for his/her customers to find someone else who is more readily accessible. Remaining where we are will cost us.

Transformational Leaders do not accept the status quo as a resting place, but a place to move forward from. They ask the questions: How can we do better? What else could we do? They are willing to disrupt the current state in order to experience transformation for the better: a better state, better performance, stronger team, better bottom-line, deeper relationship, more harmony and balance, and a stronger customer experience. These leaders understand that good is the enemy of great. They understand that when we keep doing things the same way, we limit our potential and stifle our growth. In fact, we will leave our employees, our constituents, the next generation of our leaders, and citizens with a negative impact. They understand that what we do in the present will affect the future. They recognize that maintenance does not lead to advancement. They appreciate that potential without execution is meaningless. They realize that the vision that they see must be translated into strategic, aligned and deliberate actions. They must lead in such a way, that it is seen and felt by followers. When this happens, they will see it as their own vision and commit to take action. That commitment to the vision and action is what drives the change and the realization of what is possible.

As we reflect, we see the faces of those leaders who have indeed been a transformational force for our path.

Perhaps it was a teacher, a parent, a manager, a pastor, or community leader; without whose influence, we would be in a less desirable state. In fact, without their leadership, we might have become irrelevant. Their articulation, inspiration and attention to the vision awakened us and compelled us to take actions towards a better state.

Transformational Leaders serve two critical purposes, which require courage and self-awareness:

- Awakening consciousness.

- Inspiring action.

Individually and collectively people are often operating without awareness of how they are thinking, and how that thinking is influencing their actions and behaviors. The courageous leader is usually the one who holds a mirror up for people to see themselves; to become aware of the reality of their situation and the perceptions that hold them there. The mirror also gives them a glimpse of the possibilities that anchor their hopes.

"Courage is not the absence of fear,
It is the presence of trust
In something bigger
than the fear."
-Sackeena Gordon-Jones

Essentials: Courage and Self-awareness

Long before James McGregor Burns introduced the concept in his book on Leadership, published in 1978, Transformational Leadership existed. Burns defined transformational leadership as "a process where leaders and their followers raise one another to higher levels of morality and motivation". The style or approach that the Transformational Leader uses with others is evocative and respectful; it calls for something within before requiring something outward. It demands courage and garners respect. These leaders use an approach that demonstrates vulnerability, conviction, and courage. When leaders recognize that who they are and how they show up impacts those they lead, they begin the journey of self-awareness. This requires courage, because the more we know about ourselves, the more vulnerable we feel. The effect is that we experience heightened assumptions that if others knew us, they may not like us. The danger of these assumptions is that we may unconsciously pretend to be who we are not, and lose our way.

In the 'Divine Comedy', Dante writes:

"In the middle of the journey of our life I found myself within a dark woods where the straightway was lost."

The more we pretend to be what we think others want, instead of being who we are, the more lost we become. We lose awareness of our self, and lose our way to fulfillment. Self-awareness is necessary for us to understand, appreciate, manage, and leverage ourselves in our personal and professional arenas. To see ourselves, we need to reflect and be open to the feedback of those around us. Others have a glimpse of us that we often miss. The psychologists Joseph Luft and Harrington Ingham, came up with a tool called *"The Johari Window"*. They proposed that the key to self-awareness lies in realizing that there are four window panes that provide a whole view. The four panes include: private, public, blind and unknown views. They further suggest that self-awareness is heightened as we balance between self-disclosure and constructive feedback. As leaders, we must not just be open to feedback, we must solicit it. This is where vulnerability steps in. As a pilot, we must be open to the insights of the instruments around us, and those that are watching from the towers outside of us. The insights of others Leaders have abilities, but they also need help.

This can be a little unsettling, and perhaps cause a bit of fear.

The *"likability"* and *"failure"* factors rise up to meet us, and we find ourselves coming face to face with vulnerability. This can be a showstopper. If we allow it, it will weaken us, hold us back, and even paralyze us. There are different ways in which we can see vulnerability.

In Computer Science, vulnerability is the intersection of three elements:

* A system susceptibility or flaw.

* Attacker access to the flaw.

* Attacker capability to exploit the flaw.

Brene Brown in her book: *'Daring Greatly: How the courage to be vulnerable transforms the way we live, love, parent, and lead'* defines the humanistic perspective of vulnerability as *"uncertainty, risk and emotional exposure"*. The tendency for most leaders is to take the computer science perspective. We try to hold back if not eliminate vulnerability. This shows up in our tendency towards perfectionism. We do not want to be susceptible to flaws. One concern might be that our teams, staff and or constituents will see flaws and exploit them. We do not consider that this type of exploitation causes a lose-lose situation. If this scenario plays out, it's likely that the leader loses credibility and the team loses momentum. This sort of negative thinking keeps us in stress mode, rendering us less effective. This pattern creates a self-fulfilling prophecy, allowing our vulnerability to get in the way of our performance. What is necessary here is that we face our vulnerability with courage. We cannot have courage where there is no fear. Courage is not the absence of fear, but the willingness to move forward in the face of it. Courage enables us to open the windowpanes, learn what we need to, and become better because of it. This is the arena of self-development, in which we all need to play.

President Roosevelt's speech *"Citizenship In a Republic"* includes a fitting quote: *"It is not the critic who counts; not the man who points out how the strong man stumbles, or where the doer of deeds could have done them better. The credit belongs to the man who is actually in the arena."*

The Transformational Leader embraces opportunities for self-awareness and self-development. Self-awareness is heightened through introspection as well as feedback. There is a common saying: *"feedback is the breakfast of champions"*, so a leader must not skimp on breakfast. Sometimes the feedback comes from those outside of the team and may not be constructive. Other times, it comes through circumstances and results that speaks clearly to the leader. Such is the case with the social media channels today; feedback comes fast and at times furious. The leader is vulnerable here, and must face the situation with courage, coupled with grace.

Leaders need to meet constructive feedback with conscious and deliberate leadership development. Development in the past usually meant taking classes, but such is no longer the case. In the last decade individualized development has proven effective.

Coaching, individual and small group leadership and executive development, are now key components of the best leadership development programs. These approaches to development offer a focused and customized solution and yields unprecedented results. Transformational Leaders engage in coaching for themselves and apply the concepts of coaching with the people that they lead. When the leader incorporates a coaching style, we see Transformational Leadership at its best. Coaching provides a deliberate, intense, and sincere intervention that leads to the most powerful awakening: the revelation of who we are presently and the potential of all we can be. Transformational Leaders want this for themselves, and they want to provide it to those they lead. This is not to suggest that Transformational Leaders are professional coaches. They have simply found the way to lead using coaching techniques. They do less telling and selling; and more developing and empowering. We see this coach-like approach in action, within the book of Genesis; used by the ultimate leader. After Adam sinned, God has an intervention with Adam; the Holy Scriptures reflects He used a "coaching approach": Inquiry versus

Telling. God asks: "Adam, where are you?"[1] This would be what a coach would refer to as a 'powerful question' in that it required Adam to reflect and gain deeper insight of his being. This was not a geographical question. It was a question to facilitate self-awareness and new insight. It was not about where he was physically in the garden, but where he was spiritually and philosophically, in his relationship with God and himself. The inquiry called for reflection and introspection on his thinking, as well as, his present and future state. What was his leadership role? How was he delivering on the expectations? The idea, as Burns puts it, is to inspire to higher levels of morality and motivation. Transformational Leaders often spend time in solitude, using those moments for reflection and deep consideration. These captivating leaders, revel an interest in others that comes to the forefront. They partner with other to develop their potential and draw out the Transformational Leader within them. This approach to leadership helps to close gaps, and right wrongs, in service of humanity flourishing. It fosters an environment of empowerment and mutual respect. There are situations that require different styles of leadership; the effective

---

[1] Gen 3:9-11

[2] National Women's Business Council I nwbc.gov

leader is agile in varying among the styles. I offer the following view of coaching in the context of this topic: *"Coaching is a facilitative relationship between a coach and person being coached (coachee), that takes a holistic approach to fostering spiritual, mental and behavioral insights. This brings the coachee to a "moment of truth" or awakening, which compels him/her to see and act differently in service of liberating their potential and achieving meaningful goals. The International Coach Federation (ICF) defines coaching as partnering with clients in a thought-provoking and creative process that inspires them to maximize their personal and professional potential".* Coaching is not about telling someone what they need to know or do; nor is it about offering someone advice, based on the coach's/leader's expertise or experience. Coaching is about helping a person to become conscious or awakened to where they are, how they're thinking, and who they're being. In essence, coaching heightens awareness. This helps the person gain insights and perspectives that propel them forward. Ultimately coaching enables a person to see/think/behave in ways that are congruent to their goals, values and potential. This shift and action enables a person to accomplish meaningful goals and achieve their desired results. In his book, entitled *AHA,* Kyle Idleman, refers to it as *'Awakening Honesty and Action'*.

Autocratic Leadership may have its place; and as some say: it may have had its day. What we are seeing in the 21st century is that people are not looking for leadership that exercises power and dominance, often for their own benefit. On the contrary, they are embracing the style of leadership that at its essence, reflects the capacity to see an ennobling vision, translate it into goals and inspire others to see the alignment of their potential and desires in it. This type of leadership advocates a better future, which often means a change in situation or circumstances; while fulfilling the purpose and or destiny of others.

Transformational Leadership is getting others to work and live together towards and for mutual objectives. When each person is on a course to maximize his or her own potential in service of a shared vision, we experience win-win-win situation. The resolve, aspiration and energy of the team, makes the vision possible and leads to its accomplishment.

In the Harvard Business Press work entitled: *'Handbook of Leadership theory and Practice'*, the observation made of Transformational Leaders is that they are inspiring, morally uplifting, and focused on developing followers into leaders.

Steve Denning, in his work on "The Leader's Guide to Storytelling", cites several characteristics and approaches of Transformational Leaders. For example, these leaders exhibit strong values and ideas, and are effective at motivating followers to act in ways that support the overall good. This leadership style involves a process whereby an individual engages with others and creates a connection that raises the level of motivation and morality in both. A few leaders in the recent century come to mind; In the social arena: Mandella, Gandhi and Martin Luther King. In the business arena: Mary Kay Ash. In the sports and life arena: Coach Landry, Coach Wooden and Coach Smith. These leaders influenced their followers to dream big, discover and cultivate their potential and to experience their unique destiny, while influencing transformations along the way. Each age in our history reflects that transformational leaders have stepped up with courage and self-awareness, giving rise to a better experience for all of us.

THE ART OF TRANSFORMATIONAL LEADERSHIP

What appeals to us about Transformational Leadership are both the quality of the leader and the expression of their style: They will not rattle off these characteristics as a list describing themselves, instead it will be what you experience of them. You will not only notice what they do, but also how they make you feel.

Certain competencies and characteristics are paramount to their role. This leader will align what they believe, say and do. The Transformational Leader has a clear voice. A clear voice requires clarity of one's values, beliefs and priorities. It is only through this clarity that a leader can stand and lead authentically. This authenticity is the key to the art of leadership. The artist has the ability to challenge and excite us. The skilled artist also has the ability to transform us from where we are into another space or another time and invites us to see possibilities. The transformational leader uses a dynamic canvas to do the same thing. Three overriding competencies are recognized in the artistry of the Transformational Leader:

Agility

The leaders' agility enables them to excel in the midst of uncertainty, chaos and fear. We reflect on the simple definition of agility as the ability to be quick and graceful. Organizations, communities and countries are facing tremendous change at rapid speed. Conditions in nature, culture, and the marketplace are shifting in ways that are unpredictable at times. The more we grow and advance, the more we realize how much we do not know. These variables call for leaders who have mental and relationship acuity. The ability to sense what wants to happen, while bringing focused energy on what needs to happen is paramount. The ability to take in what is present and draw conclusions quickly, while gracefully including others are manifestations of agility. Like the paint pallet and the seaside landscape in the artists' space, the Transformational leader mixes volatility, uncertainty, complexity, and ambiguity and paints a picture that calls us forward. The leader must be fluid, focused and yet agile. This suggests a leader who is open to learning, even in the midst of chaos, while being sensitive to people and situations. They are able to think quickly and operate decisively in the midst of a changing landscape.

Integrity

A leaders' integrity is a critical component as it speaks to a need that followers have: knowing what to expect. Are their behaviors congruent with their words. I suggest a perspective on integrity that is not necessarily linked to morality, but to integration or completeness. A leader's ability to demonstrate congruency, leads to trust; which is a factor crucial for leadership to be transformational. Transformational leaders demonstrate uncommon integrity; it is about the relationship they have with themselves: That their intellectual, physical, philosophical, and mental aspects are integrated. This enables others around them to not show up compartmentalized but with the freedom to be whole. These leaders are able to withstand the limelight, because they are who they are; and people become so acquainted with them that they connect. This connectedness undergirds the relationship that followers have with their leader fuels their ability to achieve extraordinary feats together. The passion and energy that the leader brings colors the canvas and reflects the artists' way and drive: integrating the people and elements to create something definitive that makes everyone's experience better.

Along with agility and integrity are personal characteristics that support the leader in bringing about transformation. Let us consider the following four that leaders regardless of their industry, whether in corporate, health care, or public sector, throughout history demonstrate:

Personal Characteristics

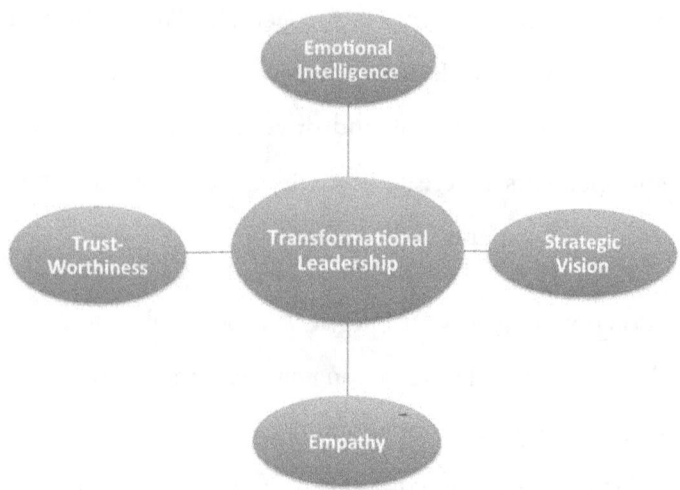

The leader has a strategic vision. They see something that is possible. This vision becomes the driving force because it is what compels us to engage ourselves fully with the leader. They see a future that's better than our present. They speak of that future so graphically, that we see ourselves in it. Consider what Martin Luther King conveyed: A day when regardless of race, culture or gender, our children will sit together as people. People from all backgrounds and ethnicity were compelled to move towards that vision.

The leader will be able to communicate empathy.

We are not speaking here of someone who is overly emotional are sympathetic. However, what we will notice is a leader who understands or seeks to understand our vantage point. They can communicate empathetically and offer us acknowledgement. This sincere acknowledgement gives reasonable space for sharing and consideration of new perspectives. A stronger strategic relationship is built not just based on "tell and do", but on multiplied synergies and feelings of being heard and seen.

Trustworthiness is a characteristic that is not easy to develop, but necessary for leadership success.

Trust is necessary for sustainable results and linked to retention, engagement, innovation, and accountability. People will not stay, play, or take your breath away, if they do not trust you. According Pat Lencioni, author of "The five dysfunctions of a team", if there is an absence of trust, the very results the leader seeks are threatened. Trust is a factor of two variables that the leader must demonstrate; character and competence. The leaders' character must reflect integrity, congruence of the hips and the lips (walk the talk). In addition, the leader must demonstrate competence; the knowledge, ability and capacity to lead in their space. In short, leaders build trust with both their know and their how.

Emotional Intelligence (EQ), which is the ability to know and manage one's self, while giving regard to those that we interact with. This is gaining momentum today as it transitions from the reference of a 'soft skill' to a 'hard skill'. EQ is often cited and found to be one of the primary causes of executive derailment in a study done by the Center for Creative Leadership. It is also a critical factor today in government, as we see world leaders fail because of a lack of EQ. Today's leader must connect the dots between who they are and how they are showing up. They must manage their emotions, while understanding and dealing with the emotions of others. The emotionally intelligent leader knows who they are, what their triggers are, what emotions they are experiencing and why-in short they are self-aware. Added to that they know how to manage their emotions. For example, they do not allow feelings of disappointment, to lead to an outburst of tears, or yelling at a team member. They are able to demonstrate self-control and self-regulation. As a result, team members do not have to wonder if they can step into the office today without the leader barking at them. Emotional Intelligence is also about social awareness and regulation. The leader demonstrates an understanding and appreciation for others, embraces diversity and is culturally conscious and respective. The Transformational Leader reflects self-awareness and discipline, consideration of others, and the ability to lead with people in mind. As a result, they radiate positive energy. They energize, encourage, and strengthen those under their leadership.

As the artist invites colors to dance on the canvas, so the leader invites these characteristics and competencies to dance on the canvas of our organizations and cultures. These leaders are acutely aware of what is happening in and around them. They are instinctively drawn toward the "burning platform", and when there, they arouse consciousness in others.

They play to their strengths and leverage the strengths of others, creating a zone where purpose, potential, partnership, values, and ethics meet. In this space, they dance.

We have seen this type of leadership during the 20th century in notable community and world leaders. In the 21st century, we have seen corporate and non-profit leaders who have worn this mantle. Though few and far in-between, they are powerful and memorable. The name of Steve Jobs and Malala Yousafzai may come to mind.

Consider India gaining their independence. The citizens did not wage a violent war. They were resolved that a change needed to take place and they were led by a Transformational leader. Gandhi held forward a powerful and empowering strategic visionary, driven by a burning platform. The possibilities of millions were ignited toward a better future. They did something unprecedented and achieved what was far-reaching, but possible.

Consider the end of Apartheid in South Africa. This extraordinary result was achieved, not through a violent citizen led-war, but through Transformational Leadership. The world witnessed an authentic leader with resolve, courage, self, and social awareness; and we watch as he gained the trust of those in and outside of his domain. His leadership inspired others to leverage their potential to achieve a better state for millions, and ultimately changing the course of nations.

Consider the Civil Rights Movement in the USA. Accomplishing this feat required Transformational Leadership. The world watched as a transformational leader emerged. He communicated clearly, what would be the burning platform that demanded action. He articulated an inspiring vision, which compelled others, to not only own it, but to be willing to die for it. The history of the United States changed forever, and the destiny of millions turned around. Imagine all the lives of multiple races totally transformed.

Consider corporate leaders of the 21st century like Steve Jobs and Lou Gerstner. They exhibit the qualities of transformational leaders. The level of engagement reflected by the people following these leaders was high; they were committed, energized, and innovative. They discovered their potential and unleashed it. Even in grievous situations, they rose up to the best they could be. They practiced law, discovered medicines, generated innovations that made the lives of millions better.

When you look closely, these leaders are similar. For each

of them, the status quo was the burning platform. Each had an ennobling vision; inspiring higher levels of morality and motivation. They stood for what they believe and connected with their followers in a partner like way. They communicated empathy through their words and presence. They were seen as genuine, authentic, emotionally intelligent, integrated, and ethical. People believed, admired, and respected them. Through their leadership, others were inspired to take the bold actions necessary for the achieving meaningful goals.

"Every Transformation Begins with a Shift"

-*Sackeena Gordon-Jones*

THE PRACTICE OF TRANSFORMATIONAL LEADERSHIP

Transformational Leadership is fueled by Coaching.

A Coach helps you see what you don't want to see, hear what you don't want to hear, do what you don't want to do, so that you can become what you always knew you could be -
--Coach Landry

The coaching style will be a dominant factor seen in Transformational Leaders. Their belief in the people they lead, evokes this style as it lifts people to discovering and unleashing their best selves.

In his work on Situational Leadership, Ken Blanchard notes that there are stages in which a leader must coach, in order to achieve desired results and performance.

Leaders who incorporate coaching into their style and behaviors garner results, as well as, respect and trust.

Transformational Leadership is a practice where behaviors, attitudes, characteristics and competencies are demonstrated daily. These practices are ingrained in people who have embraced this type of leadership. Their character, their style, their vision, their very purpose demands the dynamic, people-binding, moral lifting, conscious arousing transformations that they evoke.

CRITICAL CHARACTERISTICS

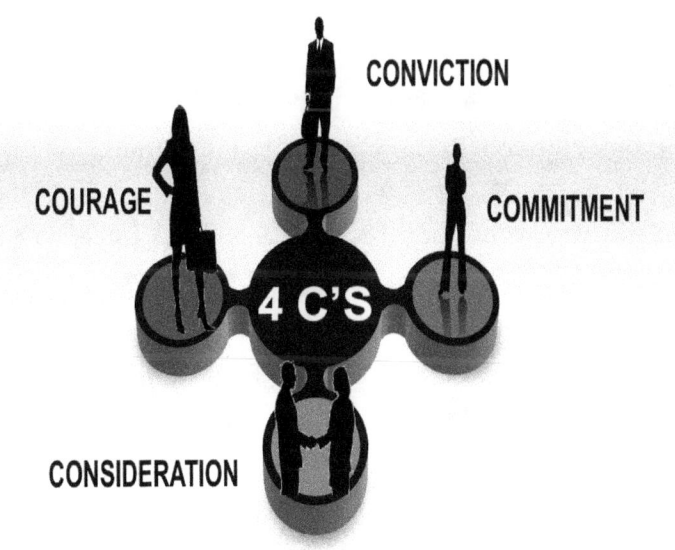

The Four Cs of Transformational Leaders

Conviction

Transformational Leaders have conviction; strong beliefs that they passionately believe in and principles that they hold to. The vision that they see is aligned with their conviction, as are their core values. Like the mothers in the MADD organization, conviction propels leaders' actions. When asked "what keeps you up at night?" the answer for many transformational leaders will lie in their convictions. Convictions harness a leaders' motivation and compels them to stand and take action for what they believe. Their drive is contagious, drawing others to share their pursuit. In fact, at times the conviction of the leader becomes the conviction of the followers or team.

In this way, conviction becomes a unifying force; and a unified force is a formidable opponent.

In fact, convictions are often the foundation for vision. It makes the vision sustainable, regardless of circumstances. The leader never lets go of the vision because it is rooted in their convictions.

Commitment

It is clear to see that 'integrity' and 'conviction' would lead to commitment. Transformational leaders engage and follow through on their promises. They hold themselves accountability, and because of this, build trusted relationships. The cause, the vision, the people that they support will get their attention, at times to the exclusion of everything else. Transformational leaders are committed to bringing out the best in their teams or followers. They encourage others by their dedication to the organizations' mission or their cause. These leaders are so devoted that they are willing to get "dirty"; they show up, not just with words, but also with actions. They are committed to themselves first: knowing and being who they are. They take on the burden of obligation for the cause or mission, and stand shoulder to shoulder with their team or followers. So powerful is their commitment, that this too becomes a source of inspiration and influence on others.

Consideration

They are concerned about the well-being of their people. With their people focused orientation, these leaders are inclined to provide human support, as well as, structural support. They attend to the making of provision to address the basic needs (food, rest, shelter), as well as, the higher level of actualization needs of their employees or constituents. When a leader provides a reasonable salary and work schedule, they show concern that the basic needs of their people are being fulfilled. When they provide leadership and wellness coaching opportunities, they show that other actualization needs are important as well. Providing for team building, employee development, performance review and salary increases, are just a few ways that leaders demonstrate consideration in attending to the human needs. Transformational leaders in organizations will also create structures to support their people. Structures will include such things as role definition, performance expectations, knowledge management practices, and recognition programs to name a few. They consider that to bring out the best of people, they need to provide access to information, resources, and appropriate incentives. This means that policies like performance management, cannot be status quo, but must evolve to meet the emergence of the needs of their people, as well as, their organizations vision.

Courage

Whether it is on the battlefield of a military leader, the client negotiating room of an entrepreneur or the boardroom of the corporate leader, courage is a crucial component of Transformational Leadership. Courage can be defined as, *"The quality of mind or spirit that enables a person to venture out, or persevere in the face of difficulty, danger, the unknown, or fear with bravery."* Many leaders today are far from courageous. The politics in government and organizations have stymied their leadership. Fear of the unknown, or in some cases, the known, has led them to keep their heads down and follow along in order to survive. In essence, aborting their Transformational Leadership potential. This phenomenon has given rise to internal conflict and high levels of stress, rendering many in a leadership position as impotent. This results in more transactional leadership; management of the status quo. However, courage is the cornerstone of a transformational leader, who has vision and is on fire with their purpose.

They stand on a 'burning platform', and they see the lives of countless others on that platform as well. Courage emboldens him or her to stand up for their convictions, to consider others and to commit to a cause for the good of many. The leader who takes responsibility for a decision made, demonstrates courage. Likewise, moving forward the agenda of the vision, in the face of opposition or threats, reflects courage. The leader who says what needs to be said, to whom it needs to be said, demonstrates courage. Righting wrongs, acknowledging contributions and empowering others to achieve and be more, requires courage. Leading from the front, not just pointing to the way; also going the way, are the mark of courage. When what we know needs to happen, compels us, in spite of the opposition or challenges; we reject status quo and step forward toward what is possible – that is courage. It is courage that fuels our creativity, makes visible our possibilities, ignites our actions, and builds our momentum.

The practice of Transformational leadership suggest ongoing activities in which we get better and better. The word practice is defined as; "the actual application or use of an idea, belief, or method as opposed to theories about such application or use". There are numerous classes and theoretical works about transformational leadership. Yet, if those studies and readings are not transferred into the marketplace, the community, the legislative office, and other organizations; we will all be left with the status quo.

We've considered the personal and critical characteristics that are embodied in the Transformational leader. The leader must seamlessly demonstrate these characteristics in their life. They do this in an authentic way, not as tools, but as the essence of who they are.

Two Key Perspectives

To become proficient at the practice of Transformational Leadership requires embracing dual perspectives. The first is *'being'*; which refers to the character. While we are tempted to define our leadership by our 'doing', the deeper and more impactful aspect is our *'being'*. To practice our *'being'* requires awareness, receptivity, and consciousness. There must be times of quietness or even silence, to allow the leader to 'be'. To sit with oneself, in quietness or reflection gives rise to insight and an experience of awakening that you can take into your work. This experience from reflection gives birth to a *'knowing'*; which the ancient Greek philosophers saw as a crucial principle: *"Know thyself"*. Transformational Leaders embraced the journey of finding themselves; of knowing who they are being. They understand that, who they are, and why they are, are intricately connected. The peace that they have is in knowing that there is a reason for their existence. They realize they were destined to be born and designed for a purpose. They matter and their leadership matters. The greater the consciousness they experience, the stronger the quality of their *'being'*.

These leaders are not just open to feedback, they live on it. After all, "feedback is the breakfast of champions". The *"Johari Window"*, reminds us that self-awareness, is expanded by receiving feedback from the perspective and insights of others. Opening up to the feedback and perception of others, increases one's clarity of how they are showing up, as well as, allows them to have a deeper connection to their people. This connection fosters trust and encourages transparency. When people feel that they know the leader and resonate with his/her being, they are more likely to support and follow the leader. In essence, the leaders' credibility and relationship currency increases, giving way to expanded possibilities. The relationship currency carries sustainable weight; it enables others to join the leader in taking the leap off the burning platform.

"For as a man thinks, so is he"

Neuroscience, informs us that when we know more about ourselves, we improve our metacognition. Metacognition is about knowing how we think.

This suggests that Transformational Leaders think about how they think:

- Where are my thoughts coming from?

- What has framed my reference?

- How did I come to that assumption?

This higher functioning thinking enables leaders to successfully navigate through complexity, ambiguity, and opportunity. Leaders with high levels of metacognition are able to communicate in ways that increase understanding and reduces conflict. They help others to examine how they are thinking, and in so doing, expand their effectiveness. This level of effectiveness translates into a perception of competence; and thereby increases the credibility of the leader and the *'trust factor'*. People connect and believe in this type of leader. When a leader arrives at this stage, their presence is commanding, and their energy is contagious. At this stage a leader voice, is true and clear; they are a voice and not an echo. They have a point of view, and are not simply replaying someone else's message. Their character and values are seamlessly woven into their personhood, so that we do not just see them, we feel them.

We want to touch them, because they touch us.

Leaders, who want to increase their self-awareness, sometimes seek out the use of specialized assessments, engage with a professional coach, and spend some quiet time in reflection. Knowing who you are and why you are, inspires you 'to be who you be'. Being who you are implies Authenticity. This suggests honest relationships, alignment to values, and an ethical foundation.

The second perspective for the transformational leader is 'doing'. This is the arena of competence. Competence is defined as, "the ability to do something successfully or efficiently". Corporations spend millions of dollars each year, to provide their leaders with knowledge acquisition programs. Leaders leave workshops and retreats with large notebooks that proves that they had access to knowledge. In addition, bookshelves and social media rooms are stocked with books, articles and blogs; all providing knowledge. However, without the ability to transfer that knowledge into action, a leader is not able to be effective. The gap between knowing and doing is of the biggest challenges facing companies, organizations, and governments. It creates frustration and disillusionment, which hinders progress. One of the reasons this gap exists is that leaders get insufficient practice. An opportunity to put what they know into practice is necessary; and the space for doing so must be somewhat safe. If a leader attempts to put something in practice and fails at doing so, how does the organization or the constituents respond? If failure is usually met with punishment or disdain, then leaders will refrain from practicing. A leaders' fear of failure becomes an obstacle to transformation. Imagine what would happen if our babies were punished when they took a step and fell. What would happen if they did not summon up the courage to try again? Would they ever walk? Transformational Leaders know what to do: they must transfer that knowing into doing. In short, they must walk the talk. Words to live by, are just words, unless we live by them.

As mentioned before, EQ is a crucial competence and one that influences the "doing". EQ is more than self-awareness. It also encompasses self-management. The awareness side is the 'knowing', while the management side is about the 'doing'. When a leader couples knowing with doing, he or she reflects EQ. Sometimes we find a leader who uses his/her knowledge about their personality style, as an excuse. For example, a leader may say: "I can't help that I make decisions based on logic, not emotions". This leader overlooks the fact that people are affected by decisions and must be given consideration, for the decision to have the desired impact. Instead, the Transformational leader will use the self and social awareness coupled with self-management and regard for others. Then we would likely see the scenario play out differently: This leader would use metacognition and social awareness to make a decision that is not just based on his/her preference, but considerate of those who will be effected. When leaders fail to use, emotional intelligence, their leadership is not sustainable. In fact, this critical component has made popular the term: "getting in their own way". This has become increasingly essential, because EQ or a lack there of, does not only impact the leader, it also impacts the followers. EQ influences morale, creativity, collaboration, and productivity. The fact is that bottom line results are linked to EQ. What a leader does creates a feeling and people are impacted, motivated and empowered by how they feel. Maya Angelou said, "people may not remember what you did, but they will remember how you made them feel".

In their work *"The Leadership Challenge"* Kouzes and Posner state that there are five practices (behaviors that are performed habitually) of exemplary leadership; and I would submit, each are congruent with the practices of Transformational leaders.

Consider the following practices of Transformational Leaders:

Model the way. This suggests authenticity and congruence between stated values and actions.

Inspire a shared vision. Communicating a picture of the future that connects with others and is compelling.

Challenge the process. Moving beyond the status quo and striving for innovation and what is better.

Enabling others to act. Developing others through training, coaching and delegating.

Encouraging the heart. Recognizing the value and

effort of others and communicating that genuinely.

These practices coupled with the aforementioned characteristics, paint a picture of the leader who works from the inside-out. Transformation begins mentally, engages the entire being, and explodes through physical action.

"Be transformed by the renewing of your mind..." Rom 12:2

The transformational leader inspires, as a necessity, to cause the people that they lead to breathe and celebrate. Inspiration is more than an emotional experience; it's essential in a physiological sense. The more we learn about brain-body work, the greater our awareness of the impact of inspiration. Inspiration in a literal sense is about breathing. The physical action of breathing promotes physiological impacts that build capacity. Neuroscience now validates that breathing exercises decrease stress and increase cognition. The transformational leader will ensure structures and processes that provide sufficient down times and times of encouragement; knowing that this will lead to greater creativity, productivity and momentum. This also creates a strong sense of community and renewed energy to continue the journey and the work.

"If our actions inspires others to dream more, learn more, do more and become more, then you are a leader"
-John Quincy Adams"

BECOMING MORE OF A
TRANSFORMATIONAL LEADER

Transformational leaders lead from the inside out.

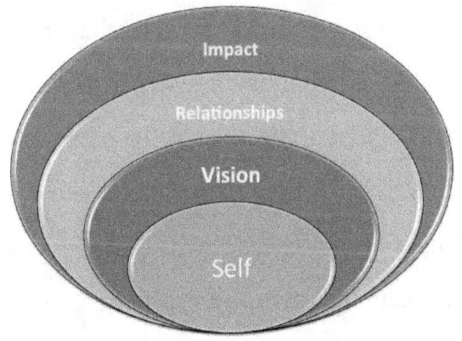

The four levels of leadership depicted in the graphic above are causally linked. Essentially the first three levels require the leader's attention to drive the fourth, the impact. Becoming a transformational leader is a process. The first step in the process is to understand the one person we can change. This of course means that the journey begins when the leader is ready to become introspective. When a leader come to terms with his/her self, they are liberated to make a sustainable impact. and it begins within. So the first step in the process begins with self.

Self

Know Your Talents, Strengths, Gifts, Values, Triggers, and Style

We are all created with unique talents that are linked to our purpose. It is important to note that talents and gifts are indicators of what we are here to do. Talents are natural enablement that we can develop and strengthen through practice. Gifts are divine enablement; which we are to develop and strengthen through spiritual maturity. Identifying our talents and creating opportunities to develop them, will enable them to become strengths. Strengths, as explained by Marcus Buckingham, are not the things you do well, but the things that you do, near perfect, and are instinctively drawn to.

Values are the things that are important about your conduct, whether at work or home. If 'authenticity' is a core value for you, you want to show up that way in the office. If your role calls you to be inauthentic, it will cause you stress and impact your performance. If your family expects you to be what you're not, living at home becomes stressful as well. For that reason, the values of a leader are reflected in their behavior and decision making.

Style refers to the personal preferences of how the leader gets energized, structures themselves, communicates and thinks. Styles are necessarily wrong or right, they are just different. When a leader can operate in their style, it makes the work easier; sort of like writing with your left or right hand. The Myers Briggs Type Indicator (MBTI) Assessment is a tool many leaders use to better understand their style.

Triggers are quite important for the leader to manage his/her self. Triggers go hand and hand with EQ. They are the stimulus that initiates a series of reactions, internally and externally. When a leader understands their triggers they can set boundaries to reduce, if not eliminate, the conditions that would lead to the triggers.

Understand your purpose

Our purpose is the life force that gives meaning and ultimately leads to greater fulfillment. When we are on purpose, we can breathe. When we are working and being in concert with our purpose, it is like taking a meditative intentional deep breath in and exhaling in the same fashion. It is invigorating and restorative. According to Kevin McCarthy, "Our purpose answers the 'why' question"; it is our reason for being.

Develop and release your potential

Potential is often hidden, and requires action on our part. You must connect with the source of your potential. Then understand your purpose, which will enable you to express your talent and continually practice it. Perfecting it requires practice and you will likely experience some failure. Remind yourself that failure is part of the development process. If you learn from it, you fail forward. Potential is ability that is not yet distinguishable, and capacity that is not yet visible or apparent.

Grow your capacity

Your capacity is the container for your potential. If your container is small, you will not be able to release your potential. You will undoubtedly play small. Your container may be the organization that you are in, and/or the role that you play. It is the reason that sometimes, you have tension in an organization that others may be comfortable in. You can feel the tension, because your potential is bigger than the container can hold. If you plant an acorn in a deck pot, it will grow. However, it will experience tension after a while and show signs of distress. Ultimately it may die, unfulfilled. If you grow the capacity, by taking it out of the pot, and planting it in the yard, it will be able to reach its potential.

Clarify your priorities

If you do not know what you stand for, you will fall for anything. Understand what you believe and why. Declare your intentions, and then give attention to your intentions. Your priorities should be reflected in your calendar, in your spending, in your relationships, and in your health. What will you give precedence to? Priorities are negligible when purpose or values are not know.

Know the Vision and Mission

Every organization needs a mission statement to provide the context for what they do. Without a mission statement, people show up but are nebulous about what they are really achieving. This is a critical component for a leader to convey; it is painful, if not impossible to lead people, without a clear mission. Without a vision, there is no mission. If people do not know where we are going, then what they are doing has no context and may lack meaning. The mission serves the following critical functions:

- It clarifies the focus and direction in alignment to the purpose. Transformational leaders use mission statements to remind their employees or followers why their organization exists, and what they need to accomplish. In essence, it serves as a "North Star" that keeps everyone moving forward with gazelle-like focus on his or her activities.

- It provides the rationale for decision-making. It provides guidance and boundaries, which gives way to a frame of reference; which support the thoughts and decisions being made.

Build and maintain relationships.

This includes the people you partner with, the people that you lead, and the people that you affect by your leadership. The results that you deliver are driven and sustained by relationships.

Relationship currency is the driving asset inside an organization.

This is the reason that interpersonal skills are crucial. Relationships are based on how two or more people regard and relate to each other.

Influence everyone else.

The relationship from within the organization effects the relationships created outside the organization. How a leader relates to their team influences how their people relate to customers or constituents. The ability to drive customer satisfaction often rests on this factor.

Impact

The fourth element, essential to Transformational Leaders, is an outcome of the first three: impact. Everything the leader does affects the impact that they make. This impact eventually translates into the brand and reputation of the leader and their organization. How the leader manages self, carries out their mission, and builds relationships contributes to an impact that is bigger than any one person. It is this impact that makes a difference for an office, and organization, a community, a nation and generations. Consider the impact of Steve Jobs. None of us sees a phone how our grandparents did. Consider the impact of Mother Teresa. None of us can stand by and see the hunger and pain of others without doing something to help. Consider the impact of Dr. Charles Richard Drew, an African-American physician who developed ways to process and store blood plasma in "blood banks". Saving the lives of our military would not have been possible to the degree that it was in WWII without this. Leaders with a vision impact literally impact generations. Consider the impact of Mary Kay Ash on women and the beauty industry. She set out to run a company where people were treated with respect. A priority for her was to encourage women to unleash their potential. The impact was women working from home raised their economic wealth to the millionaire status and changed the face of successful business owners. Today, women-owned firms have an economic impact of $3 trillion that translates into the creation and or maintenance of 23 million jobs, 16 percent of all U.S. jobs[2].

---

[2] National Women's Business Council I nwbc.gov

Shift Happens!

Coaching and Leadership

The demands of leadership have created a need for that the field of Coaching has satisfied. The leader benefits from a strategic partner, who can help them in real time, to be at the top of their game. The coach provides an arena to support the leaders' transformation by facilitating a creative process that maximizes their personal and professional potential. Coaching, once thought of only in the sports arena, has transcending into every arena over the past couple of decades. Coaching is the process that respects both people in the relationship and genuinely seeks the flourishing of the person being coached. The power to transform starts with facilitating an empowering mindset. Leaders, who have been coached, find ways to create a "coaching culture" in their organization. This dynamic creates a ripple effect that enables the leader to achieve extraordinary results through people who are maximizing their potential. In essence, through coaching, the leader facilitates the transformation of possibilities into realities.

The coaching leader, creates a high performing team, commonly referred to as "a dream team", by doing four things well:

1. Aligning people to the vision

2. Unleashing the potential of others

3. Providing feedback and Inspiration

4. Fostering accountability

They believe that people are their greatest asset. *"What we believe influences who we are and that in turn impacts everything we do"* – Gary Collins. If this is true, then the central focus of coaching will be to tap into beliefs and radically create shifts that start in the mind. *"Be transformed by the renewing of your minds"*. -Rom 12:2

The fostering of accountability is a crucial factor for the transformational leader. Lack of accountability will end in poor or no results. People often mistake intention for action. They have intention to do something, but never quite get around to it. Intentions can become lost in the face of challenges and circumstance outside of one's control. Those who achieve sustainable success, do so because they are accountable not because they have intention. Intention without action is a wish; and wishes do not often lead to accomplishments. Action is the seed of accomplishment, and accountability is the fuel of action. Tom Smith and Roger Connors offer a fitting definition of accountability in their book: *"The Wisdom of Oz"*: *"a personal choice to rise above one's circumstances and demonstrate the ownership necessary for achieving desired outcomes"*. Leaders, who do not foster accountability with their people, end up with an epic problem known as *'Monkey Management'*. This is when leaders take on the work that their people should accomplish, which results in overworking and other negative repercussions.

Monkey Management Negative Repercussions
Burn Out

They work twice as hard, doing their work, and the work of others. Driven by their passion for the vision, they assume the work necessary and absolve their people of their responsibility.

The leader expends all their energy and end up physically and mentally exhausted and often emotionally stressed.

This stress leads at times to undesirable results, which create a cycle of stress:

- Less time with family and as a result the loss of family relations

- Eating uncontrollably or unwisely. As a result, disease sets in the body

- Diminished thinking capacity. As a result, they make poor decisions and form negative habits.

Myopically Focused

When leaders lose their strategic focus, the vision, as well as, their leadership starts to fail. They become so focused in the weeds; they can no longer see what is happening to the garden. A leaders' edge is lost when they loose focus of the vision or the strategic landscape.

They lose sight of their relationship with people. People lose their value and become objectives that create pain and toil for them. They speak harshly, listen less, and judge quickly. This erodes the trust that was previously establish and creates a dynamic that pulls them further into this behavior.

Coaching is a vital link to eradicating *'Monkey Management'*, which stands in the way of sustainable results. Coaching brings out the best in others, and fosters accountability. By using coaching skills, leaders keep theirs and their peoples' attention and energy where it will do the greatest good.

The Transformational Leader must master the *"soft skills"*. Ironically, what has been termed "soft skills" (people skills), has proven to be the "really hard skills". Leaders who use a coaching style, find it easier to recognize and appreciating differences, as well as, leveraging the creativity and strengths of others. Coaching leaders create an environment where everyone contributes based on strengths aligned to the vision, accomplish goals and create impact, faster, smarter and better.

Coaching helps the leader keep their eyes on what is important. What happens if a leader misses the opportunity to leverage the strengths of those on their team?

They interfere with potential and can sabotage the personal mission of their people, which will likely become an obstacle to the leaders' mission.

The following story depicts how this sort of thing could occur in the animal kingdom.

"Many years ago, the animals in the Great Forest decided that they wanted to start a school for all their children. Until that time, it had been the responsibility of parents to teach their children the skills that they needed to know, but the animals in the Great Forest wanted their children to learn from professional teachers. Therefore, they organized a school and hired staff.

The teachers met and decided to provide a standardized educational curriculum to their animal students. Therefore, they adopted an activity curriculum consisting of swimming, running, flying, and climbing. All the animals took all the subjects – because it was very important to them that no animal be different. To ensure that animals were progressing satisfactorily, standardized achievement tests were administered to all animals.

Here is what happened. The ducks were excellent in swimming. In fact, the ducks were better than their teacher. However, some of the ducks made only passing grades in flying and all of them were very poor in running. Since they were slow in running, they had to stay after school for remedial running practice, and they had to drop swimming in order to practice running during their swimming class time. This was kept up until all the ducks' webbed feet were very sore. In addition, the ducks were so tired, that soon they were only average in swimming. However, average was acceptable in school, so nobody worried about that – except the ducks.

In running, the rabbits started at the top of the class, but they did very poorly in swimming. In addition, the rabbits insisted on hopping around, and the teachers were concerned about their hyperactivity – so they made the rabbits walk everywhere instead of allowing them to run or hop. The rabbits had to come in early every day for special swimming class. Many of the younger rabbits developed severe fur problems because they had to spend so much time in the swimming pool.

The squirrels were excellent in climbing and running. In fact, the squirrels were the best students at climbing the standardized tree. They wanted to fly by first climbing the tree, then spreading their paws, and gliding to the ground (That's the way squirrels fly). But in flying class their teacher made them start on the ground instead of at the tree top, and the squirrels were not mastering the course material. So every day, the squirrels had therapy - a flying therapist took the squirrels into the gym and made them do front-paw exercises to strengthen their muscles so they could learn to fly the right way. The squirrels' paws hurt so much from this overexertion that some of them only got a C in climbing. Some of the squirrels failed climbing altogether.

The eagles were definitely problem children – in climbing class, the eagles beat all the others to the top of the tree, but they insisted on using their own way to get there and were quite stubborn about it. The eagles said that clearly, it was the goal that mattered, and that it was quite right for eagles to get to the tree top by flying. The school psychologist diagnosed them as having oppositional-defiant disorder. A strict behavior modification plan was developed for the eagles."

As Transformational Leaders, we do not try to make

everybody the same, we want everybody to fulfill their God-given potential with their strengths, passions, gifts, and talents in service of a vision for our collective good. The truth is when support people in maximizing their potential, we maximize possibilities for all of us. This is how visions are realized, and legacies are made.

"It's not the man that makes the vision; it's the vision that makes the man."
Mahatma Gandhi

LET'S DO THIS

We need Transformational Leaders to help guide us and propel us to live an abundant, meaningful, enjoyable and fulfilling life. How do these leaders move us forward? They inspire us, they model authenticity, they challenge empower, and encourage us. They use varying leadership styles and they incorporate a 'coaching' approach. They bring out the best in us; for the betterment of ourselves and those around us.

Transformational Leadership is not for a few elite or special men and women. It is for all of us, to bring forth the best from us and create communities where we can all thrive. We may not all lead organizations, but we can all lead: ourselves, family and our community.

Transformational Leadership has emerged as not just the style of choice, but also the leadership style of necessity. The shift from leader-focused to follower and relationship focused has resulted in epic impact in past centuries: We have seen changes in organizations, communities, countries and continents fueled by men and women who were authentic, visionary, courageous and transformational. They engaged others in a strategic vision for the good of all. They used their strengths and abilities to inspire others to move beyond personal interests to a more ennobling vision and pursue it, even with their lives. Transformational leaders don't just "talk the talk", they also "walk the talk"! It's important to note that both the talking and the walking are crucial. Leaders hold crucial conversations. These conversations are pivotal, in that they create space for meaningful dialog that stirs up the awareness or consciousness of others. In this space we people hear and are heard. Thoughts are discussed in a way that facilitates learning and gives birth to shifts. These shifts create new paradigms, new hopes and new realities. Reflecting on the contributions of the Transformational Leaders in our lives, it is quite clear, they have facilitated paramount shifts which have propelled us to live better, work smarter, respect and leverage our differences, build better communities, lead our organizations and governments more effectively.

The secret is out. Transformational Leadership is within your reach. You will release your potential for leading by reaching inside of you. Dare to discover what you believe firmly, what you are passionate about and what you are called to affect. Let that vision become your legacy, and everyone you touch, will be better for it.

"A leader has the vision and conviction that a dream can be achieved. He inspires the power and energy to get it done."
Ralph Lauren

REFLECTION QUESTIONS

1. Which transformational leaders have affected your life? Past or Present?

2. What do you consider the essential characteristics and behaviors of a transformational leader?

3. What impact does the characteristics and behaviors of Transformational leader have on you as a person, and as a follower?

4. What is the value of a leader with a clear vision?

5. How does a Transformational Leader:
   a. Build trust
   b. Develop rapport
   c. Improve performance
   d. Impact retention
   e. Drive execution

6. If you had absolute trust in your leader, how would that impact:

   a) Your performance

   b) Your energy

   c) Your commitment

   d) Your potential

7. In what way are you showing up as a transformational leader? (consider your role(s) at home, work and in the community)

8. What do you need to change to become the transformational leader you are called to be?

9. More specifically, what do you need to:
    • Start

    • Stop

    • Do Differently

10. What support do you need?
    ☐ Mentor
    ☐ Coach
    ☐ Counselor
    ☐ Consultant

It all starts with a Vision: What do you see yourself contributing to? What are you inspired to impact or transform? Next comes your Calling: What are you uniquely called/qualified/purposed for? When the Vision and Calling are clear, the Transformational leader emerges. All leaders are born. All leaders have a purpose to which they are called. All leaders have a vision; what they see with their mind's eye, that doesn't exist, but certainly needs to.

11. What do you see? (write the vision)

Every leader must be clear on these 6 Facets:

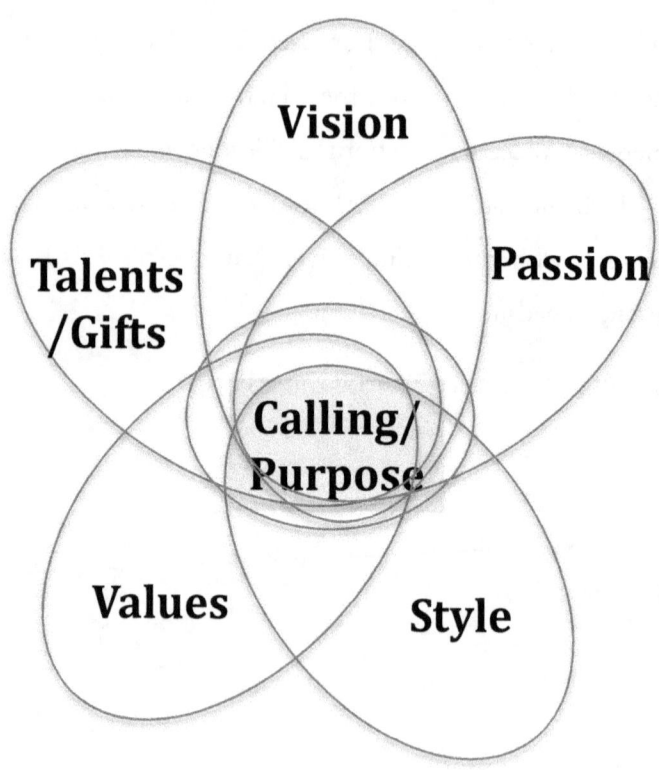

Now that you have your vision, take time to reflect and answer the following questions:

12. Passion: What do you care deeply about? What are you inspired to impact and transform?

13. What are your unique combination of talents & gifts? What activities do you engage them in that strengthen you?

14. What are your core values?

15. What is your personal and/or personality style?

16. What do you feel you are specifically called to do to live out your purpose?

Transformational leaders leave behind a living legacy. They believe in continuous learning, and help others to grow and move forward.

17. What will you leave behind?

RESOURCES AVAILABLE AT:
WWW.TRANSFORMATIONEDGE.COM

VISION MAPPING	THE COACHING LEADER
A Vision Board helps you see where you want to be, but a Map provides you with insights for the path to your destination. This interactive workshop enables you to develop a customized "roadmap" that transforms your visions, goals, and dreams into your reality. Go from seeing it, to being and experiencing it.	This experiential workshop provides awareness and development of the essential coaching skills for leaders. It equips those responsible for the development, performance, and feedback of others with the tools, techniques, and best practices to integrate coaching into their leadership style.
AUTHENTIC LEADERSHIP	**TRANSFORMATIONAL CHRISTIAN LEADERSHIP**
Leaders who find their voice, live their values, and have a compelling vision, even in the face of complexity and uncertainty; create an empowering organization, where talent thrives and they accomplish extraordinary results. This program includes a leadership assessment and follow-on coaching.	For Ministry Leaders This workshop identifies the practices of transformational leaders and helps participants build the practices and capacity to lead their ministry, develop leadership and purpose driven disciples with Christian principles.

ADDITIONAL RESOURCES A:
WWW.TRANSFORMATIONEDGE.COM

COACHING SERVICES

EXECUTIVE & LEADERSHIP COACHING

- Coaching and assessment services for senior executives
- Coaching for women in leadership
- Coaching for emerging leaders and front-line managers
- Coaching for high potentials
- On boarding/transition coaching

TEAM & GROUP COACHING

- Leadership and Matrix team coaching
- Group coaching for women in the C-Suite, Business owners and nonprofit leaders
- Group coaching for ICF Coach Credentialing
- Team coaching for Boards

TRANSFORMATION EDGE
COACHING & CONSULTING

GLOSSARY

Transformational
A condition of instability or danger, as in social, economic, political, or international affairs leading to a decisive change.

Coaching
Partnering with clients in a thought-provoking and creative process that inspires them to maximize their personal and professional potential.

Fuel
Something that sustains or encourages; stimulant.

Philosophy: The rational investigation of the truths and principles of being, knowledge, or conduct.

Congruity
A quality of agreement and appropriateness. When there is congruity, things fit together in a way that makes sense.

Conviction
Strongly held, principled beliefs.

Leadership
A process of social influence, which maximizes the efforts of others, towards the achievement of a goal.

ABOUT THE AUTHOR

 Sackeena is the Chief Coaching Officer for Transformation Edge, the leading Coaching, and Consulting practice for leaders and organizations, who want to transform the way they think, lead, work and live.

An expert in the coaching field, Sackeena serves as the director of the Business Coaching Certificate Program at NC State University in partnership with the Business Coach Institute. She has served as two-time president of ICF –Raleigh and led the chapter to two international awards: "Breaking Barriers" and "The Gift of Coaching".

Sackeena specializes in leadership coaching and works with executives and leaders who aspire to unleash their potential and create sustainable impact in their organizations and community, while leading a life that is in harmony and balance with their values and purpose.

Sackeena has served as the Global Head of Learning and Development; strategic advisor, management consultant, leadership development specialist and studied strategy and change management, human development and behavior, neuroscience of coaching, organizational effectiveness and holds a PhD in Leadership studies.

When not working, Sackeena enjoys the beach, and moments with her family. Her favorite quote currently is *"Moments Matter"*.